To our wives:
Margi and Tammy.
Special people God
placed with us.

ISBN: 1-56476-047-2

Cover design: Joe DeLeon
Editor: Liz Duckworth
Production: Myrna Hasse, Kristine Smith

1 2 3 4 5 6 7 8 9 10 Printing/Year 97 96 95 94 93

·IN·THE·PICTURE·WITH·JESUS·

PEOPLE AND PLACES

WRITTEN BY TOM SIEMS

ILLUSTRATED BY SCOTT ARBUCKLE

VICTOR BOOKS

A DIVISION OF SCRIPTURE PRESS PUBLICATIONS INC.
USA CANADA ENGLAND

FIND THESE FACES

Look for Jesus and His twelve disciples in each story. If you look carefully, you should find them all. Of course, we don't know what they *really* looked like. But the artist has helped us picture each one on these pages—both front and side views.

Have fun with the stickers in the back of the book. Imagine yourself in the story. Would you have been standing next to Jesus? In the front of the crowd? Looking out a window? Sitting in a boat? Put a "Me" sticker in that spot and think about what you would have seen, heard, and felt. Add to the pictures with other stickers. Make each picture your very own.

JESUS

JAMES

JAMES THE LESS

THADDAEUS

ANDREW

TROUBLE IN THE TEMPLE

John 2:12-16

Jesus was in Jerusalem for the yearly Passover celebration.

As He walked into the temple to pray, Jesus looked around and began to get angry. Noise and dust filled the temple air. Some men were selling cattle, sheep, and doves. Others sat at tables exchanging money.

These money changers were cheaters who traded money for temple coins to buy the animals. They traded unfairly and kept a lot of the money they collected for themselves.

Jesus became even more angry. Quickly He made a whip out of rope. CRACK! The whip snapped and popped! The sheep and cattle stampeded.

CRASH! Jesus overturned the tables where the money changers sat. Their coins flew across the room.

Then Jesus yelled, "Take these things out of here! Don't you ever turn My Father's house into a place to make money!"

Do you worship God first, or do other things get most of your time and energy?

MARTHA

Luke 10:38-42

Jesus and His disciples came to a village named Bethany. There a kind woman named Martha welcomed them into her home.

Martha got busy getting supper ready, while her sister Mary sat on the floor near Jesus. She sat still and listened carefully to what Jesus said.

Soon Martha grew worried about all the work to be done. So she burst into the room saying, "Lord, don't You care that my sister has left me to get everything ready by myself? Tell her to come and help me!"

But Jesus answered gently, "Martha, Martha, you are worried and bothered about so many things. But only one thing is really needed. Mary has chosen the best part, and it must not be taken away from her."

What worries keep you from thinking about Jesus?

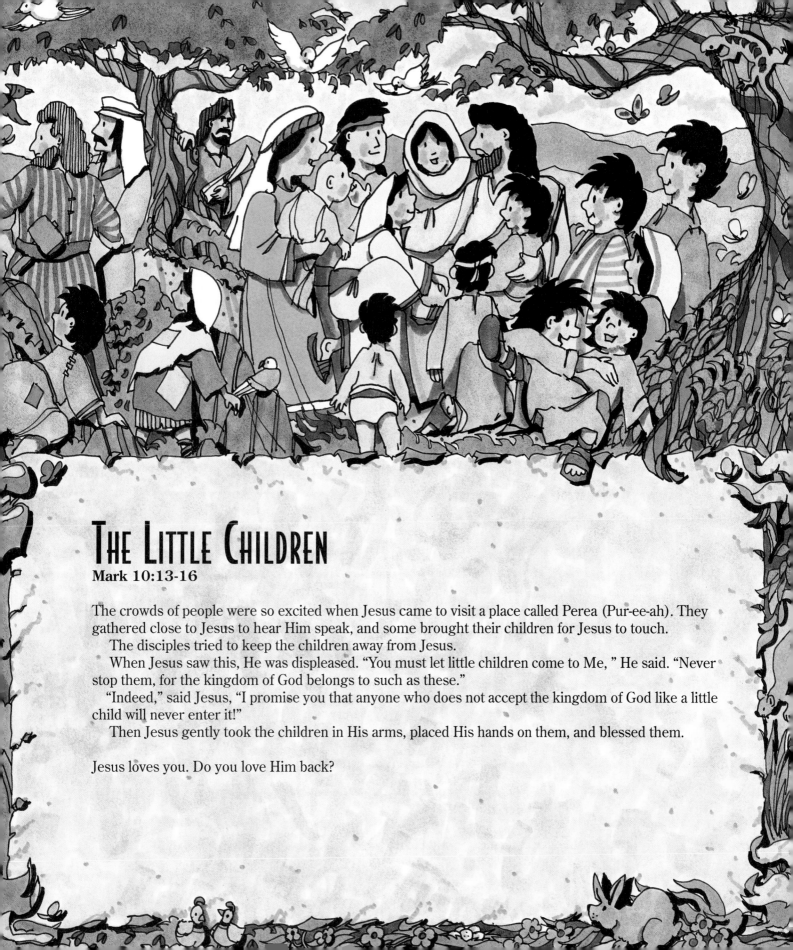

THE LITTLE CHILDREN

Mark 10:13-16

The crowds of people were so excited when Jesus came to visit a place called Perea (Pur-ee-ah). They gathered close to Jesus to hear Him speak, and some brought their children for Jesus to touch.

The disciples tried to keep the children away from Jesus.

When Jesus saw this, He was displeased. "You must let little children come to Me, " He said. "Never stop them, for the kingdom of God belongs to such as these."

"Indeed," said Jesus, "I promise you that anyone who does not accept the kingdom of God like a little child will never enter it!"

Then Jesus gently took the children in His arms, placed His hands on them, and blessed them.

Jesus loves you. Do you love Him back?

The Religious Leaders

Matthew 22:34-40

In Jerusalem the religious leaders thought they knew more about God than Jesus did. They wanted to ask Jesus some tricky questions that might get Him in trouble with the leaders of the country.

Each time they tried, though, Jesus was one step ahead of them. His answers were always just right.

Finally, one of the experts who had studied God's Word asked, "Master, what is the greatest commandment?"

People in the listening crowds held their breath and leaned closer to hear Jesus' answer. How could He ever choose from so many important commandments?

Jesus answered calmly, " 'Love the Lord your God with all your heart, and with all your soul, and with all your mind.' This is the first and greatest commandment. And there is a second like it: 'Love your neighbor as yourself.' All of God's important laws depend on these two commandments."

Once again, Jesus surprised the people with His wisdom and understanding.

How can you show love to God and to others?

THE RICH YOUNG RULER

Mark 10:17-27

A man knelt at Jesus' feet. "Good Master," he asked, "what must I do to be sure I'll live forever?"

"You know the commandments," Jesus answered. "Do not kill. Do not be unfaithful. Do not steal. Do not lie. Do not cheat. Honor your father and mother."

"Master," the young ruler said, "I have carefully obeyed all these since I was a boy."

Jesus looked closely at the man. "You need one more thing. Sell all you have. Give the money to the poor. Then you will have riches in heaven. And then come back and follow Me."

The man went sadly away, because he had lots of money and didn't want to give it up. Jesus said to His followers, "It is easier for a camel to go through an eye of a needle than it is for a rich man to get into God's kingdom."

"Then who can possibly be saved?" they asked.

Jesus answered, "With men it is impossible. But all things are possible with God!"

Would you give up everything to follow Jesus?

Zacchaeus in the Tree
Luke 19:1-10

"I want to see Jesus!" Zacchaeus said to himself. He was a rich man—a tax collector who often cheated people.

When a crowd gathered to watch Jesus enter their town of Jericho, Zacchaeus—who was very short—could not see over the heads of all the people there. Not one to give up, he climbed a tree to get a better view.

When Jesus came near, He called out, "Zacchaeus, come down! I must be your guest today."

Zacchaeus jumped out of the tree and gladly welcomed Jesus. But some people in the crowd started muttering, "Now Jesus has gone to visit a very wicked man!"

Little Zacchaeus was so happy that Jesus wanted to spend time with him that he promised, "I will give half my property to the poor. And if I cheated anyone, I'll pay them back four times as much!"

Jesus knew that Zacchaeus would be different from now on. After all, it was the wicked people that needed changing. Jesus told His new friend, "It is the lost I've come to seek—and save."

How has your belief in Jesus changed the way you act?

THE POOR WIDOW IN THE TEMPLE

Mark 12:41-44

Clink! Clank!

The coins rattled at the bottom of the offering cups in the temple at Jerusalem.

Jesus watched as people dropped their coins into the large boxes. Many rich people put in large sums of money.

Then a poor widow came by. The woman dropped in two little coins, worth less than a penny.

When He saw this, Jesus called to His disciples. "Believe Me, this poor widow has given more than all the others. They have dropped in what they can easily afford to give. But this woman is poor and needs so much. Yet she has given all she owns—everything she has to live on!"

Can you trust God to provide you with all you need?

MARY OF BETHANY

John 12:1-8

The whole house was filled with the sweet smell of perfume! Jesus was in Bethany visiting His friends Mary and Martha and their brother Lazarus.

While Martha prepared supper, Mary took a bottle of expensive perfume and poured it over Jesus' feet. Then she wiped His feet with her long hair. She wanted to honor Jesus in this way.

One of Jesus' disciples, Judas Iscariot, cried out, "Why on earth wasn't this perfume sold and the money given to the poor? It's worth thousands of dollars!"

Judas didn't say this because he cared about the poor, but because he was a thief. He had stolen money from the other disciples.

Jesus told Judas, "Leave Mary alone! She has saved this for the day of My burial. You have the poor with you always—but you will not always have Me."

Mary wanted to give Jesus a special gift. Do you give your best to Jesus?

PONTIUS PILATE

Matthew 27:11-26

Because they were jealous and afraid of Jesus' power, some evil men had Jesus arrested.

They brought him before a leader of the Roman government—Pontius Pilate. This leader could decide if Jesus was guilty, or he could set Jesus free.

Now, during this certain time each year, one prisoner was released if the people chose him. The other prisoner was named Barabbas, and he was a bad man.

Pontius Pilate gathered the people and asked them, "Who should I set free? Jesus or Barabbas?"

The evil priests told the crowd to ask for Barabbas. So the people shouted, "We want Barabbas! Punish Jesus!"

Pilate did not want to lose control of the mob of people. So he washed his hands in a bowl of water—right in front of the people—and said, "I am innocent in this decision. It is your responsibility. Set Barabbas free."

Pilate released Barabbas and had Jesus beaten and nailed to a cross.

Soon after, Jesus died on the cross. He rose from the dead three days later! He lives today! Let's be glad that God can even use evil people to bring good to the world.

Do you choose Jesus today?

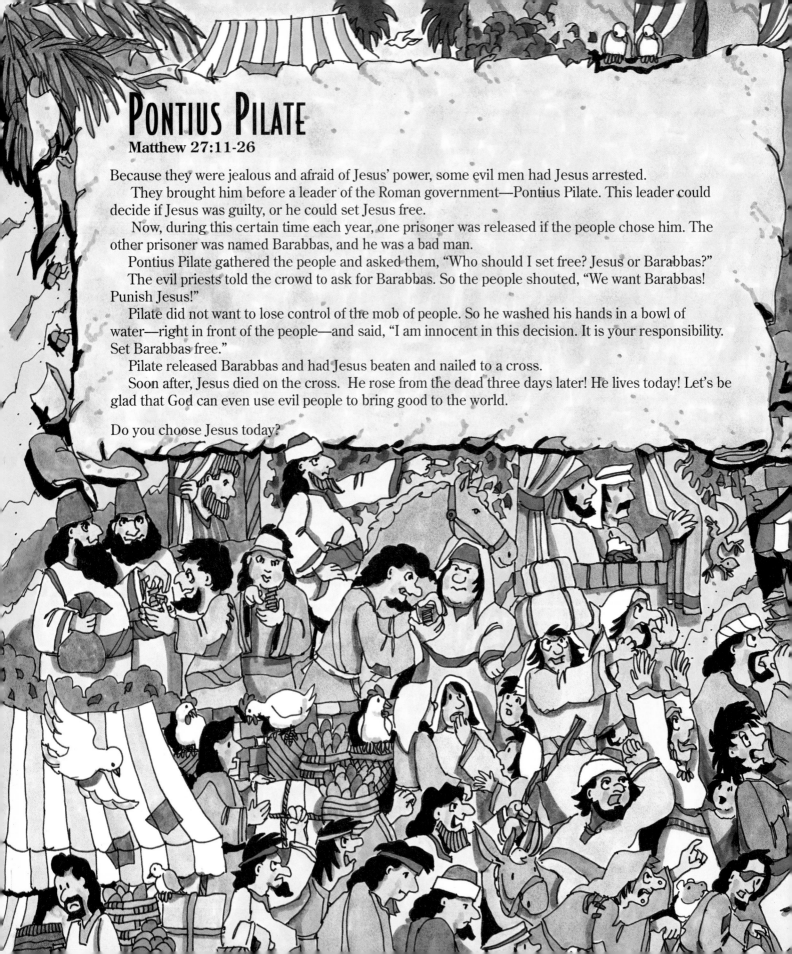

FOLLOW ME FURTHER: A DISCUSSION GUIDE

How many people do you think Jesus met face to face? Why was it so many people wanted to see Jesus? He performed miracles and was also a great teacher. But what makes Jesus Christ different from all other men is that He is God's Son. He is the Messiah, the Savior who came to seek and save the lost!

Jesus had two principle tasks while He was here on earth: (1) to live a perfect life of obedience to God, and (2) to die on the cross for our sins, so that all who believe in Him will have everlasting life (see John 3:16). As you study these stories of people and places, you will learn more about Jesus. We hope all who read this book will also know Him as Savior and Lord. Jesus wants you to live like Him: putting God first and loving others!

Trouble in the Temple (John 2:12-16)

Lesson: Jesus cares about the holiness of God's house.

1. Why do you think animals were being sold in the temple? (Some of the people who went to Jerusalem for Passover needed to buy animals to give to God as sacrifices. It was easier for people to buy animals from the money changers than to carry them while they traveled.)

2. What did Jesus mean by "My Father's house"? (Jesus' Father is God. And God's house [or the temple] is where people go to worship and praise God.)

3. Why was Jesus angry at the money changers? (They thought it was more important to make money than to worship God. They cheated people and kept the money for themselves. Be sure not to put anything ahead of God. Worship only Him.)

Martha (Luke 10:38-42)

Lesson: Take time to listen to Jesus.

1. Jesus said, "Mary has chosen the best part." What is the best part? (Mary chose to listen to Jesus' teachings instead of worrying about getting things ready for all the guests. Jesus is the best part. Seek Him first!)

2. What was Martha doing? (She was worrying about the chores. While we need to take time to do our chores, Jesus teaches that it is more important to listen to Him and obey His words. Are you listening to what Jesus has to say to you in the Bible?)

The Little Children (Mark 10:13-16; also see Matthew 19:13-15; Luke 18:15-17)

Lesson: Accept Jesus with childlike faith.

1. Why was Jesus angry with His disciples? (They were holding back the children that wanted to come to Jesus. We should never block anyone from getting to know Jesus.)

2. What did Jesus do when He held the children in His arms? (He laid His hands on them and blessed them. This loving action by Jesus shows that His blessing is freely given to those who trustingly receive it. Jesus loves you too. Though He doesn't put His hands on you, you can be sure He is always there, watching over you.)

3. What did Jesus mean when He said "the kingdom of God belongs to such as these"? (We don't get

into God's kingdom by our own works or good deeds. Rather, it must be received as God's free gift through trusting in Jesus as our personal Savior.)

The Religious Leaders (Matthew 22:34-40; also see Mark 12:28-34; Luke 10:25-37)

Lesson: Jesus gave these two great commandments: (1) Love God, and (2) Love others.

1. What did Jesus say are the two greatest commandments? (Jesus said they are "love the Lord with all your heart, and with all your soul, and with all your mind" and to "love your neighbor as yourself." We should love God first, then love others who are created in God's image. By obeying these two commands, you keep all the others.)

2. Who is your neighbor? (Jesus was asked this question by a religious leader. [See Luke 10:29-37.] He answered by telling the story of the Good Samaritan who took care of a stranger in need of help. We should show love to others like the Good Samaritan.)

The Rich Young Ruler (Mark 10:17-27; also see Matthew 19:16-26; Luke 18:18-27)

Lesson: Seek God first.

1. What commandment did the rich young ruler find impossible to obey? (He kept those that tell us to love others, but could not obey the first commandment that nothing be more important to us than God. He loved money more than God. We should use our money to serve others, and remember that everything we have comes from God. What do you love more: God or other things?)

2. Is it impossible for a rich person to get into heaven? (Jesus said with God all things are possible. As long as a rich person does not love money more than God, he could still go to heaven. Are you sure that you will go to heaven to be with Jesus forever? If not, you can pray this simple prayer to ask Jesus into your life: Heavenly Father, I believe You sent Your Son, Jesus, to be my Savior. I am sinful and can only know You because Jesus died on the cross for me. I trust Jesus to forgive my sins. Jesus, I ask You to be my Savior so I can have everlasting life. Amen.)

Zacchaeus in the Tree (Luke 19:1-10)

Lesson: Jesus' love changes people.

1. What did Zacchaeus do to see Jesus? (He was so short, he climbed a tree to see Jesus over the crowd. He could have turned away, but he would not give up.)

2. Why did Jesus say Zacchaeus had been saved? (Zacchaeus showed his life was changed when he put God first and loved others. Like the rich young ruler, Zacchaeus was wealthy. But unlike the rich young ruler, Zacchaeus responded to Jesus by his changed actions. Have you shown your faith in Jesus through your actions?)

The Poor Widow in the Temple (Mark 12:41-44; also see Luke 21:1-4)

Lesson: Do your best with what you have.

1. How much did the poor widow give? (She gave two small coins worth less than a penny. However, the value of her gift should not be measured by how much she gave. Rather, it should be determined by how she gave it. The poor widow gave knowing that God would take care of her to provide her needs.)

2. Why did Jesus say the poor widow gave more than all the others? (The poor widow had very little. She gave all she owned, everything she had to live on. The others gave out of what they owned. They could afford to give more. Do you give out of gratitude like the poor widow?)

Mary of Bethany (John 12:1-8)

Lesson: Give first to Jesus.

1. What did Mary do with her perfume? (She poured it over Jesus' feet. Then she wiped His feet clean with her hair. Mary knew Jesus was about to die, and she gave her best to Jesus.)

2. What did Judas want to do with the perfume? (He said he wanted to sell it and give it to the poor. But he really wanted to keep some of the money for himself. Jesus told Judas, "You will always have the poor among you." By this Jesus didn't mean that there would be many chances to help the poor; rather, He meant there wouldn't be many more chances to show love to Him while He was still on earth.)

Pontius Pilate (Matthew 27:13-26; also see Mark 15:1-15; Luke 23:1-25; John 18:38-19:16)

Lesson: We are held accountable for our actions.

1. What choice did the crowd make when Pilate asked who he should set free? (They chose Barabbas, a known murderer, over Jesus, the Son of God. People today still make bad choices by not choosing the salvation offered by Jesus.)

2. What did Pilate do after the crowd made its choice? (He said, "I take no responsibility for the death of Jesus", and washed his hands in front of the crowd. By washing his hands, Pilate meant that he wanted to stay out of the situation. But his actions spoke louder than his words, because he allowed Jesus to be killed. Pilate was making excuses. In the same way, we should stop making excuses and start taking responsibility for our own actions.)

WHAT ELSE IS IN THE PICTURE? SEE WHAT YOU CAN FIND!

Trouble in the Temple
1. How many men are there with blue hats?
2. Where is the man riding the camel?
3. Where is the lady in the window?
4. Can you find the sheep with the curly horns?
5. Look for the man running with the bags of money.

Martha
1. Find the mouse on the sleeping man's tummy.
2. How many pieces of fruit are in the basket that the girl is carrying on her head?
3. How many boys are playing horns?
4. Can you find the 2 red birds?
5. Find the three beetles.

The Little Children
1. Find the 2 frogs.
2. Where is the man cooking a fish on a stick?
3. How many lizards can you find?
4. Find the man holding a scroll.
5. Can you find the grasshopper?

The Religious Leaders
1. Can you find the fish in the basket?
2. Look for the man with a red dot on his hat.
3. Find the man with a knife in his belt.
4. How many men have green bands on their hats?

The Rich Young Ruler
1. Find the 2 birds with red feathers on their heads.
2. Where is the man fixing his shoe?
3. How many birds can you find in the picture?
4. Where is the man holding a loaf of bread?
5. How many women are in the picture?

Zacchaeus in the Tree
1. Find the boy swinging from the tree.
2. Where is the boy feeding the horse an apple?
3. Find the man with a patch on his eye and a scar on his cheek.
4. Find the man with the crutch.
5. How many ladies are carrying baskets of fruit?

The Poor Widow in the Temple
1. Where is the man with a blindfold on?
2. Can you find the man with a basket of fish on his head?
3. Find the fat man with his hand on his belly.
4. How many soldiers can you find?

Mary of Bethany
1. How many birds are sitting on the roof?
2. Can you find the mouse?
3. Where is the man with a hammer?
4. How many trees are there?
5. Find the man playing the guitar.

Pontius Pilate
1. How many men are wearing eye patches?
2. Find the man with 1 tooth and 2 warts on his face.
3. Find the 3 lizards.
4. Where is the woman with the orange headband?
5. How many soldiers are by Jesus?

PUT YOURSELF IN THE PICTURE WITH JESUS

You can put yourself in the picture with these play-action stickers!

Use your imagination. What if you were there with Jesus and the twelve? What would it feel like to stand next to Jesus? What would you have heard and seen if you were in the front of the crowd, or up in the tree with Zacchaeus, or visiting Mary and Martha?

Put a "Me" sticker in each picture and think about being a part of the Bible story.

You can add to the pictures with other stickers, and make each scene your very own.